To

....

From

....

Footprints

One night I dreamed I was walking
Along the beach with the Lord.
Many scenes from my life flashed across the sky.
In each scene I noticed footprints in the sand.
Sometimes there were two sets of footprints.
Other times there was one set of footprints.
This bothered me because I noticed that
During the low periods of my life when I was
Suffering from anguish, sorrow, or defeat,
I could see only one set of footprints,
So I said to the Lord, "You promised me,
Lord, that if I followed You,
You would walk with me always.
But I noticed that during the most trying periods
Of my life there have only been
One set of prints in the sand.
Why, when I have needed You most,
You have not been there for me?"
The Lord replied,
"The times when you have seen
only one set of footprints
Is when I carried you."

ELLA H. SCHARRING-HAUSEN

Footprints

A PREMIER JOURNAL

Ellie Claire

gift & paper expressions

...inspired by life

As one of the most cherished poems
of the last century, *Footprints* has been lovingly
handed down from one generation to the next.
It stands as a timeless reminder that God
never leaves us, that He is as close as breathing.

As you journey through the poem and the
accompanying quotes and Scriptures, let this
journal inspire you to express your thoughts,
record your prayers, and walk with God.
And during those times when the journey
is especially trying, let this be a reminder that you can
trust God to carry you—often before you even ask.

One night I dreamed I was walking
Along the beach with the Lord.
Many scenes from my life flashed across the sky.
In each scene I noticed footprints in the sand.
Sometimes there were two sets of footprints.
Other times there was one set of footprints.
This bothered me because I noticed that
During the low periods of my life when I was
Suffering from anguish, sorrow, or defeat,
I could see only one set of footprints,
So I said to the Lord, "You promised me,

I was walking with the Lord.

Lord, that if I followed You,
You would walk with me always.
But I noticed that during the most trying periods
Of my life there have only been
One set of prints in the sand.
Why, when I have needed You most,
You have not been there for me?"
The Lord replied,
"The times when you have seen
only one set of footprints
Is when I carried you."

Walk with God

Whoever walks toward God one step, God runs toward him two.

JEWISH PROVERB

Joy is more than my spontaneous expression of laughter, gaiety, and lightness.
It is deeper than an emotional expression of happiness. Joy is a growing,
evolving manifestation of God in my life as I walk with Him.

BONNIE MONSON

How blessed are the people who know the joyful sound!
O Lord, they walk in the light of Your countenance.
In Your name they rejoice all the day,
And by Your righteousness they are exalted.

PSALM 89:15–16 NASB

May your life become one of glad and unending praise to the Lord as you
journey through this world, and in the world that is to come!

THERESA OF AVILA

Those who wait in the LORD shall renew their strength;
they shall mount up with wings like eagles,
they shall run and not be weary, they shall walk and not faint.

ISAIAH 40:31 NKJV

When I walk by the wayside, He is along with me....
Amid all my forgetfulness of Him, He never forgets me.

THOMAS CHALMERS

Jesus wants to live His life in you, to look through your eyes,
walk with your feet, love with your heart.

MOTHER TERESA

My Father's World

When I look at the galaxies on a
clear night—when I look at the incredible
brilliance of creation, and think that this
is what God is like, then instead of feeling
intimidated and diminished by it,
I am enlarged—I rejoice that I am part of it.

MADELEINE L'ENGLE

How beautiful it is to be alive!
To wake each morn as if the Maker's grace
Did us afresh from nothingness derive.

HENRY SEPTIMUS SUTTON

Above all give me grace to use these beauties of earth
without me and this eager stirring of life within me
as a means whereby my soul may rise from creature
to Creator, and from nature to nature's God.

JOHN BAILLIE

This is my Father's world;
He shines in all that's fair.
In the rustling grass I hear Him pass;
He speaks to me everywhere.

MALTBIE D. BABCOCK

The earth is the LORD's, and everything in it.
The world and all its people belong to him.

PSALM 24:1 NIV

He Leads Me

The Lord's goodness surrounds us at every moment. I walk through
it almost with difficulty, as through thick grass and flowers.

R. W. BARBER

He has shown you, O man, what is good. And what does
the LORD require of you? To act justly and to love mercy
and to walk humbly with your God.

MICAH 6:8 NIV

How vital that we pray, armed with the knowledge
that God is in heaven.... Spend some time walking
in the workshop of the heavens, seeing what God has done,
and watch how your prayers are energized.

MAX LUCADO

The LORD is my shepherd;
I have all that I need.
He lets me rest in green meadows;
he leads me beside peaceful streams.
He renews my strength.
He guides me along right paths.

PSALM 23:1–3 NLT

All the way to heaven is heaven begun to the Christian who
walks near enough to God to hear the secrets He has to impart.

E. M. BOUNDS

You will reach your destination if you walk with God.

Purpose and Meaning

I believe that nothing that happens to me is meaningless,
and that it is good for us all that it should be so,
even if it runs counter to our own wishes. As I see it,
I'm here for some purpose, and I only hope I may fulfill it.

DIETRICH BONHOEFFER

God has a purpose for your life and no one else can take your place.

Call to Me, and I will answer you, and show you great
and mighty things, which you do not know.

JEREMIAH 33:3 NKJV

If you believe in God, it is not too difficult to believe that He is
concerned about the universe and all the events on this earth. But
the really staggering message of the Bible is that this same God cares
deeply about you and your identity and the events of your life.

BRUCE LARSON

To everything there is a season,
a time for every purpose under heaven.

ECCLESIASTES 3:1 NKJV

The meaning of earthly existence lies,
not as we have grown used to thinking, in prospering,
but in the development of the soul.

ALEKSANDR SOLZHENITSYN

And we know that all things work together for good to those who love God, to those who are the called according to His purpose.

ROMANS 8:28 NKJV

Bless You

The LORD bless you and keep you;
The LORD make His face shine upon you,
And be gracious to you;
The LORD lift up His countenance upon you,
And give you peace.

NUMBERS 6:24–26 NKJV

Thank God that even when we are not worthy of His blessings,
He still loves us and bestows peace, joy, and happiness.

GARY SMALLEY AND JOHN TRENT

May the favor of the Lord our God rest upon us; establish the work
of our hands for us—yes, establish the work of our hands.

PSALM 90:17 NIV

Have you ever thought that in every action of grace in your heart
you have the whole omnipotence of God engaged to bless you?

ANDREW MURRAY

Real help comes from GOD.
Your blessing clothes your people!

PSALM 3:8 MSG

We don't have to be perfect to be a blessing. We are asked
only to be real, trusting in His perfection to cover
our imperfection, knowing that one day we will finally
be all that Christ saved us for and wants us to be.

GIGI GRAHAM TCHIVIDJIAN

God bless you and utterly satisfy your heart…with Himself.

AMY CARMICHAEL

He Walks with Me

You're blessed when you stay on course, walking steadily
on the road revealed by GOD. You're blessed when you
follow His directions, doing your best to find Him.

PSALM 119:1 MSG

And He walks with me, and He talks with me,
and He tells me I am His own. And the joy we share
as we tarry there none other has ever known.

C. AUSTIN MILES

Take your everyday, ordinary life—your sleeping,
eating, going-to-work, and walking-around life—and place it
before God as an offering.

ROMANS 12:1 MSG

May your footsteps set you upon
a lifetime journey of love. May you wake
each day with His blessings and sleep
each night in His keeping. And may
you always walk in His tender care.

Walk in all the way that the LORD your God has commanded
you, so that you may live and prosper and prolong your days.

DEUTERONOMY 5:33 NIV

Love the LORD your God, walk in all his ways, obey his commands, hold firmly to him, and serve him with all your heart and all your soul.

JOSHUA 22:5 NLT

Every Need

God wants nothing from us except our needs, and these furnish
Him with room to display His bounty when He supplies them
freely.... Not what I have, but what I do not have,
is the first point of contact between my soul and God.

CHARLES H. SPURGEON

Trust the LORD! He is your helper and your shield.

PSALM 115:9 NKJV

Be sure to remember that nothing in your daily life
is so insignificant and so inconsequential that
God will not help you by answering your prayer.

OLE HALLESBY

Be assured, if you walk with Him and look to Him
and expect help from Him, He will never fail you.

GEORGE MÜELLER

Call upon me in the day of trouble;
I will deliver you, and you will honor me.

PSALM 50:15 NIV

Jesus Christ has brought every need, every joy,
every gratitude, every hope of ours before God.
He accompanies us and brings us into the presence of God.

DIETRICH BONHOEFFER

I call on you, O God, for you will answer me; give ear to me and hear my prayer.

PSALM 17:6 NIV

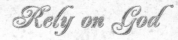

Rely on God

I saw Him in the morning light,
He made the day shine clear and bright;
I saw Him in the noontide hour,
And gained from Him refreshing shower....
I saw Him when great losses came,
And found He loved me just the same.
When heavy loads I had to bear,
I found He lightened every care....
For as each day unfolds its light,
We'll walk by faith and not by sight.
Life will, indeed, a blessing bring,
If we see God in everything.

A. E. FINN

If you are walking in darkness,
without a ray of light,
trust in the LORD
and rely on your God.

ISAIAH 50:10 NLT

It is better to walk in the dark with God than to walk alone in the light.

THE STILL SMALL VOICE

Trust in the LORD with all your heart;
do not depend on your own understanding.
Seek his will in all you do,
and he will show you which path to take.

PROVEBS 3:5–6 NLT

The LORD watches over those who fear him, those who rely on his unfailing love.

PSALM 33:18 NLT

Take My Hand

Lord, hear my prayer. When I stumble over my words, or when I can't find the right words to say, listen to my heart. I want to talk with You. I want to walk with You. Hear me, O Lord, and answer with grace and love and mercy. Take my hand and my heart and lead me.

MARILYN JANSEN

I'm still in your presence, but you've taken my hand. You wisely and tenderly lead me, and then you bless me.

PSALM 73:21 MSG

The crucified Christ is the One who comes to walk with us every day.

ANDREW MURRAY

What is important is that you are holding on, that you have got a grip on Christ and He will not let your hand go.

MOTHER TERESA

The Lord directs the steps of the godly.
He delights in every detail of their lives.
Though they stumble, they will never fall,
for the Lord holds them by the hand.

PSALM 37:2–24 NLT

As you continue holding [on], you will discover that God has a magnetic attracting quality! Your God is like a magnet! The Lord naturally draws you more and more toward Himself.

MADAME JEANNE GUYON

One took my hand at the entrance dim,
And sweet is the road that I walk with Him.

L. B. COWMAN

One night I dreamed I was walking
Along the beach with the Lord.
Many scenes from my life flashed across the sky.
In each scene I noticed footprints in the sand.
Sometimes there were two sets of footprints.
Other times there was one set of footprints.
This bothered me because I noticed that
During the low periods of my life when I was
Suffering from anguish, sorrow, or defeat,
I could see only one set of footprints,
So I said to the Lord, "You promised me,

I noticed footprints in the sand.

Lord, that if I followed You,
You would walk with me always.
But I noticed that during the most trying periods
Of my life there have only been
One set of prints in the sand.
Why, when I have needed You most,
You have not been there for me?"
The Lord replied,
"The times when you have seen
only one set of footprints
Is when I carried you."

Touching God

There is an essential connection between
experiencing God, loving God, and trusting God.
You will trust God only as much as you love Him,
and you will love Him to the extent you have
touched Him, rather that He has touched you.

BRENNAN MANNING

We desire many things,
and God offers us only one thing.
He can offer us only one thing—Himself.
He has nothing else to give.
There is nothing else to give.

PETER KREEFT

The reason for loving God is God Himself,
and the measure
in which we should love Him
is to love Him without measure.

BERNARDO OF CLAIRVAUS

Although it be good to think upon the kindness of God,
and to love Him and worship Him for it; yet it is far better
to gaze upon the pure essence of Him and to love Him
and worship Him for Himself.

I lift my eyes to you, O God, enthroned in heaven.
We keep looking to the LORD our God for his mercy.

PSALM 123:1–2 NLT

God Is with Us

God is the sunshine that warms us, the rain that melts
the frost and waters the young plants. The presence of God
is a climate of strong and bracing love, always there.

JOAN ARNOLD

Friendships, family ties, the companionship of little children,
an autumn forest flung in prodigality against a deep blue sky,
the intricate design and haunting fragrance of a flower, the
counterpoint of a Bach fugue or the melodic line of a Beethoven
sonata, the fluted note of bird song, the glowing glory of a sunset:
the world is aflame with things of eternal moment.

E. MARGARET CLARKSON

The day is done,
The sun has set,
Yet light still tints the sky;
My heart stands still
In reverence,
For God is passing by.

RUTH ALLA WAGER

We are always in the presence of God.... There is never
a nonsacred moment! His presence never diminishes.
Our awareness of His presence may falter,
but the reality of His presence never changes.

MAX LUCADO

Where morning dawns and evening fades you call forth songs of joy.

PSALM 65:8 NIV

The Majesty of God

O LORD, our Lord,
how majestic is your name in all the earth!
You have set your glory above the heavens....
When I consider your heavens,
the work of your fingers,
the moon and the stars,
which you have set in place,
what is man that you are mindful of him,
the son of man that you care for him?
You made him a little lower than the heavenly beings
and crowned him with glory and honor....
O LORD, our Lord,
how majestic is your name in all the earth!

PSALM 8:1, 3–5, 9 NIV

Forbid that I should walk through Thy beautiful world with
unseeing eyes: Forbid that the lure of the market-place should
ever entirely steal my heart away from the love of the open acres
and the green trees: Forbid that under the low roof of workshop
or office or study I should ever forget Thy great overarching sky.

JOHN BAILLIE

The God who holds the whole world in His hands
wraps Himself in the splendor of the sun's light
and walks among the clouds.

Savor little glimpses of God's goodness and His majesty, thankful for the gift of them.

Walking Together

Moments spent listening, talking, playing, and sharing
together may be the most important times of all.

GLORIA GAITHER

Dear friends, let us continue to love one another,
for love comes from God. Anyone who loves
is a child of God and knows God.

1 JOHN 4:7 NLT

You can never change the past. But by the grace of God,
you can win the future. So remember those things which will help you
forward, but forget those things which will only hold you back.

RICHARD C. WOODSOME

Let us consider how we may spur one another on toward love
and good deeds. Let us not give up meeting together,
as some are in the habit of doing, but let us encourage
one another—and all the more as you see the Day approaching.

HEBREWS 10:24–25 NIV

You will find as you look back upon your life,
that the moments when you have really lived are the moments
when you have done things in the spirit of love.

HENRY DRUMMOND

We are simply human beings, enfolded in weakness and in hope,
called together to change our world one heart at a time!

JEAN VANIER

Changed by Grace

When we focus on God, the scene changes.
He's in control of our lives; nothing lies
outside the realm of His redemptive grace.
Even when we make mistakes, fail in relationships,
or deliberately make bad choices, God can redeem us.

PENELOPE J. STOKES

There is nothing but God's grace. We walk upon it;
we breathe it; we live and die by it;
it makes the nails and axles of the universe.

ROBERT LOUIS STEVENSON

Grace is no stationary thing, it is ever becoming.
It is flowing straight out of God's heart.
Grace does nothing but reform and convey God.
Grace makes the soul conformable to the will of God.
God, the ground of the soul, and grace go together.

MEISTER ECKHART

Grace and gratitude belong together like heaven and earth.
Grace evokes gratitude like the voice an echo.
Gratitude follows grace as thunder follows lightning.

KARL BARTH

The LORD is compassionate and gracious, slow to anger, abounding in love.

PSALM 103:8 NIV

Memories of the Heart

How precious to me are your thoughts, O God! How vast is the sum of them!
Were I to count them, they would outnumber the grains of sand.

PSALM 139:17–18 NIV

Although mementos can be preserved or displayed
behind glass, memories live on in the heart,
where they deepen and resonate over the years,
providing strength and comfort in times of need.

Memory is history recorded in our brain; memory is a painter,
it paints pictures of the past and of the day.

GRANDMA MOSES

I will remember the works of the LORD;
Surely I will remember Your wonders of old.
I will also meditate on all Your work,
And talk of Your deeds.

PSALM 77:11–12 NKJV

One of the great secrets for growing up in Christ
is to remember that whether we're riding a bus
or working in the office or washing dishes at home
or playing a game of golf, Jesus Christ is there.

LEIGHTON FORD

The space between yesterday and today is filled with acceptance, forgiveness and remembering to laugh.

God's Handiwork

If we are children of God, we have a tremendous
treasure in nature and will realize that it is holy and sacred.
We will see God reaching out to us in every wind that blows,
every sunrise and sunset, every cloud in the sky,
every flower that blooms, and every leaf that fades.

OSWALD CHAMBERS

The longer I live, the more my mind dwells
upon the beauty and the wonder of the world.

JOHN BURROUGHS

Look up at all the stars in the night sky and hear
your Father saying, "I carefully set each one in its place.
Know that I love you more than these."
Sit by the lake's edge, listening to the water
lapping the shore and hear your Father gently
calling you to that place near His heart.

WENDY MOORE

Beauty puts a face on God. When we gaze at nature,
at a loved one, at a work of art, our soul immediately
recognizes and is drawn to the face of God.

MARGARET BROWNLEY

The heavens declare the glory of God;
And the firmament shows His handiwork.

PSALM 19:1 NKJV

Nearness of God

Whom have I in heaven but You?
And besides You, I desire nothing on earth.
My flesh and my heart may fail,
But God is the strength of my heart and my portion forever....
As for me, the nearness of God is my good;
I have made the Lord GOD my refuge.

PSALM 73:25–26, 28 NASB

God is not only the answer to a thousand needs, He is the answer
to a thousand wants. He is the fulfillment of our chief desire
in all of life. For whether or not we've ever recognized it, what we desire
is unfailing love. Oh, God, awake our souls to see—You are what
we want, not just what we need. Yes, our life's protection, but also
our heart's affection. Yes, our soul's salvation, but also our heart's
exhilaration. Unfailing love. A love that will not let me go!

BETH MOORE

Live in me. Make your home in me just as I do in you.... If you make
yourselves at home with me and my words are at home in you, you can be sure
that whatever you ask will be listened to and acted upon.... I've loved you the
way my Father has loved me. Make yourselves at home in my love.

JOHN 15:4, 7, 9 MSG

I will remember that when I give Him my heart, God chooses
to live within me—body and soul. And I know He really is as close
as breathing, His very Spirit inside of me.

How ow blessed is the one whom You choose
and bring near to You
To dwell in Your courts.

Loved Eternally

In some way or other we will have to learn the difference
between trusting in the gift and trusting in the Giver.
The gift may be good for a while, but the Giver is the Eternal Love.

F. B Meyer

The greatest honor we can give God is to live gladly
because of the knowledge of His love.

Julian of Norwich

For the LORD loves justice,
And does not forsake His saints;
They are preserved forever.

Psalm 37:28 NKJV

I have a home above,
From sin and sorrow free;
A mansion with eternal love
Designed and formed for me.

The impetus of God's love comes from within Himself,
to share with us His life and love. It is a beautiful, eternal gift,
held out to us in the hands of love. All we have to do is say "Yes!"

John Powell

Great is his love toward us, and the faithfulness
of the LORD endures forever.

Psalm 117:2 NIV

"God has for Christ's sake loved us." Think of it! We are loved eternally, totally, individually, unreservedly! Nothing can take God's love away.

GLORIA GAITHER

Ordinary Days

God is with us in the midst of our daily, routine lives.
In the middle of cleaning the house or driving somewhere in the
pickup…. Often it's in the middle of the most mundane task that He
lets us know He is there with us. We realize, then, that there can be no
"ordinary" moments for people who live their lives with Jesus.

MICHAEL CARD

Within each of us there is an inner place where the living God
Himself longs to dwell, our sacred center of belief.

The Word became human and made his home among us.
He was full of unfailing love and faithfulness. And we have
seen his glory, the glory of the Father's one and only Son.

JOHN 1:14 NLT

We encounter God in the ordinariness of life,
not in the search for spiritual highs and extraordinary,
mystical experiences, but in our simple presence in life.

BRENNAN MANNING

Much of what is sacred is hidden in the ordinary, everyday moments
of our lives. To see something of the sacred in those moments takes
slowing down so we can live our lives more reflectively.

KEN GIRE

If each moment is sacred—a time and place
where we encounter God—life itself is sacred.

JEAN M. BLOMQUIST

This is how we experience his deep and abiding presence in us: by the Spirit he gave us.

-1 JOHN 3:24 MSG

One night I dreamed I was walking
Along the beach with the Lord.
Many scenes from my life flashed across the sky.
In each scene I noticed footprints in the sand.
Sometimes there were two sets of footprints,
Other times there was one set of footprints.
This bothered me because I noticed that
During the low periods of my life when I was
Suffering from anguish, sorrow, or defeat,
I could see only one set of footprints,
So I said to the Lord, "You promised me,

There were two sets of footprints.

Lord, that if I followed You,
You would walk with me always.
But I noticed that during the most trying periods
Of my life there have only been
One set of prints in the sand.
Why, when I have needed You most,
You have not been there for me?"
The Lord replied,
"The times when you have seen
only one set of footprints
Is when I carried you."

God Is Near

Do you believe that God is near? He wants you to.
He wants you to know that He is in the midst of your world.
Wherever you are as you read these words, He is present.
In your car. On the plane. In your office, your bedroom, your den.
He's near. And He is more than near. He is active.

MAX LUCADO

I have sought Thy nearness;
With all my heart have I called Thee,
And going out to meet Thee
I found Thee coming toward me.

YEHUDA HALEVI

It is not objective proof of God's existence that we want but,
whether we use religious language for it or not, the experience
of God's presence. That is the miracle we are really after.
And that is also, I think, the miracle that we really get.

FREDERICK BUECHNER

The Lord is close to the brokenhearted;
he rescues those whose spirits are crushed.

PSALM 34:18 NLT

It is God to whom and with whom we travel, and while
He is the End of our journey, He is also at every stopping place.

ELISABETH ELLIOT

Draw near to God and He will draw near to you.

JAMES 4:8 NASB

Never Alone

You are never alone. In your heart of hearts, in the place
where no two people are ever alike, Christ is waiting for you.
And what you never dared hope for springs to life.

ROGER OF TAIZÉ

By entering through faith into what God has always
wanted to do for us…we have it all together with God
because of our Master Jesus…. We throw open our
doors to God and discover at the same moment
that he has already thrown open his door to us.

ROMANS 5:1–2 MSG

God never abandons anyone on whom He has set His love;
nor does Christ, the good shepherd, ever lose track of His sheep.

J. I. PACKER

When you come looking for me, you'll find me.
Yes, when you get serious about finding me and want it more than
anything else, I'll make sure you won't be disappointed.

JEREMIAH 29:13 MSG

When you take the first step to embrace God in your circumstances,
He will go the distance to embrace you.

STORMIE OMARTIAN

You are in the Beloved…therefore infinitely dear to the Father, unspeakably precious to Him. You are never, not for one second, alone.

NORMAN DOWTY

Safe Journey

He will rescue you from every trap
and protect you from deadly disease.
He will cover you with his feathers.
He will shelter you with his wings.
His faithful promises are your armor and protection.
Do not be afraid of the terrors of the night,
nor the arrow that flies in the day.
Do not dread the disease that stalks in darkness,
nor the disaster that strikes at midday....
If you make the LORD your refuge,
if you make the Most High your shelter,
no evil will conquer you....
The LORD says, "I will rescue those who love me.
I will protect those who trust in my name."

PSALM 91:3–6, 9–10, 14 NLT

We are not alone on our journey. The God of love
who gave us life sent us [His] only Son to be with us
at all times and in all places, so that we never have to feel
lost in our struggles but always can trust that God walks with us.

HENRI J. M. NOUWEN

I will lead them home with great care. They will walk beside
quiet streams and on smooth paths where they will not stumble.

JEREMIAH 31:9 NLT

God has not promised us an easy journey, but He has promised us a safe journey.

WILLIAM C. MILLER

Open Our Hearts

God can pour on the blessings in astonishing ways
so that you're ready for anything and everything,
more than just ready to do what needs to be done.

2 CORINTHIANS 9:8 MSG

God did not tell us to follow Him because He needed our help,
but because He knew that loving Him would make us whole.

IRENAEUS

The "air" which our souls need also envelops all
of us at all times and on all sides. God is round about us in
Christ on every hand, with many-sided and all-sufficient grace.
All we need to do is to open our hearts.

OLE HALLESBY

GOD made my life complete when I placed all the pieces
before him.... GOD rewrote the text of my life when
I opened the book of my heart to his eyes.

PSALM 18:20, 24 MSG

I don't know what the future holds,
but I know who holds the future.

E . STANLEY JONES

Let the beloved of the LORD rest secure in him,
for he shields him all day long, and the one the LORD
loves rests between his shoulders.

DEUTERONOMY 33:12 NIV

*Have confidence in God's mercy, for when you think
He is a long way from you, He is often quite near.*

THOMAS à KEMPIS

Always There

We need never shout across the spaces to an absent God.
He is nearer than our own soul,
closer than our most secret thoughts.

A. W. TOZER

God is always present in the temple
of your heart…His home. And when you
come in to meet Him there, you find that
it is the one place of deep satisfaction
where every longing is met. Always be in a state
of expectancy, and see that you leave room
for God to come in as He likes.

OSWALD CHAMBERS

How could I be anything but quite happy
if I believed always that all the past is forgiven,
and all the present furnished with power,
and all the future bright with hope.

JAMES SMETHAM

GOD'S love…is ever and always, eternally present
to all who fear him, making everything right for them
and their children as they follow his Covenant ways.

PSALM 103:17–18 MSG

*God wants to be wanted, to be wanted enough that we are **ready**,*
predisposed to find Him present with us.

DALLAS WILLARD

God With Us

God gets down on His knees among us;
gets on our level and shares Himself with us.
He does not reside afar off and send
diplomatic messages, He kneels among us....
God shares Himself generously and graciously.

EUGENE PETERSON

Christ will make his home in your
hearts as you trust in him.

EPHESIANS 3:17 NLT

God loves to look at us, and loves it when
we will look back at Him. Even when we try
to run away from our troubles...
God will find us, bless us, even when
we feel most alone, unsure.... God will
find a way to let us know that
He is with us in this place, wherever we are.

KATHLEEN NORRIS

When all is said and done, the last
word is Immanuel—God-With-Us.

ISAIAH 8:10 MSG

My Presence will go with you, and I will give you rest.

EXODUS 33:14 NIV

The best of all is, God with us!

JOHN WESLEY

Nothing Can Separate Us

Who shall separate us from the love of Christ? Shall trouble
or hardship or persecution or famine or nakedness or danger
or sword?... No, in all these things we are more than conquerors
through him who loved us. For I am convinced that neither
death nor life, neither angels nor demons, neither the present
nor the future, nor any powers, neither height nor depth,
nor anything else in all creation, will be able to separate
us from the love of God that is in Christ Jesus our Lord.

ROMANS 8:35, 37–39 NIV

The grace of God means something like: Here is your life.
You might never have been, but you are because the party
wouldn't have been complete without you.
Here is the world. Beautiful and terrible things will happen.
Don't be afraid. I am with you. Nothing can ever separate us.
It's for you I created the universe. I love you.

FREDERICK BUECHNER

The word of the LORD is right and true;
he is faithful in all he does.
The LORD loves righteousness and justice;
the earth is full of his unfailing love.

PSALM 33:4–5 NIV

When I feel most alone, I draw comfort from the promise that nothing can separate me from the love of Christ. Nothing. He is with me always.

Trust God

We are to simply trust God. While we trust, God can work.
Worry prevents Him from doing anything for us....
The peace of God must quiet our minds and rest our hearts.
We must put our hand in the hand of God like a little child,
and let Him lead us out into the bright sunshine of His love.
He knows the way out of the woods. Let us climb up into His arms,
and trust Him to take us out by the shortest and surest road.

PARDINGTON

You can trust God right now to supply
all your needs for today.
And if your needs are more tomorrow,
His supply will be greater also.

Ask and you'll get; seek and you'll find;
knock and the door will open.
Don't bargain with God. Be direct.
Ask for what you need.

LUKE 11:9 MSG

So faith bounds forward to its goal in God,
and love can trust her Lord to lead her there;
upheld by Him my soul is following hard,
till God hath full fulfilled my deepest prayer.

F. BROOK

*What is the Lord saying? There's only one message:
"Trust Me. Even when you don't understand and can't comprehend: trust Me!"*

JAMES DOBSON

Seek God

My goal is God Himself, not joy, nor peace,
Nor even blessing, but Himself, my God.

L. B. COWMAN

God longs to give favor—that is, spiritual strength
and health—to those who seek Him, and Him alone.
He grants spiritual favors and victories, not because
the one who seeks Him is holier than anyone else,
but in order to make His holy beauty and His great
redeeming power known.... For it is through
the living witness of others that we are drawn
to God at all. It is because of His creatures,
and His work in them, that we come to praise Him.

THERESA OF AVILA

Seek the LORD your God, and you will find
Him if you seek Him with all
your heart and with all your soul.

DEUTERONOMY 4:29 NKJV

It is God's will that we believe that we see
Him continually, though it seems
to us that the sight be only partial;
and through this belief He makes us always
to gain more grace, for God wishes to be seen,
and He wishes to be sought, and He wishes
to be expected, and He wishes to be trusted.

To seek God means first of all to let yourself be found by Him.

Faithful Guide

God, who has led you safely on so far,
will lead you on to the end.
Be altogether at rest in the loving holy
confidence which you ought to have
in His heavenly Providence.

FRANCIS DE SALES

Guidance is a sovereign act. Not merely does
God will to guide us by showing us His way…
whatever mistakes we may make, we shall come safely home.
Slippings and strayings there will be, no doubt,
but the everlasting arms are beneath us;
we shall be caught, rescued, restored.
This is God's promise; this is how good He is.
And our self-distrust, while keeping us humble,
must not cloud the joy with which we lean
on our faithful covenant God.

J. I. PACKER

He…guided them by the skillfulness of his hands.

PSALM 78:72 NKJV

Trust the past to the mercy of God, the present
to His love, and the future to His Providence.

AUGUSTINE

All the paths of the LORD are lovingkindness and truth
To those who keep His covenant.

PSALM 25:10 NASB

One night I dreamed I was walking
Along the beach with the Lord.
Many scenes from my life flashed across the sky.
In each scene I noticed footprints in the sand.
Sometimes there were two sets of footprints.
Other times there was one set of footprints.
This bothered me because I noticed that
During the low periods of my life when I was
Suffering from anguish, sorrow, or defeat,
I could see only one set of footprints.
So I said to the Lord, "You promised me,

I was suffering from anguish, sorrow, defeat.

Lord, that if I followed You,
You would walk with me always.
But I noticed that during the most trying periods
Of my life there have only been
One set of prints in the sand.
Why, when I have needed You most,
You have not been there for me?"
The Lord replied,
"The times when you have seen
only one set of footprints
Is when I carried you."

Joy and Strength

Our hearts were made for joy. Our hearts were made to enjoy the
One who created them. Too deeply planted to be much affected by
the ups and downs of life, this joy is a knowing and a being known
by our Creator. He sets our hearts alight with radiant joy.

WENDY MOORE

For you make me glad by your deeds, O LORD;
I sing for joy at the works of your hands.

PSALM 92:4 NIV

If one is joyful, it means that one is faithfully living for God
and that nothing else counts; and if one gives joy to others one
is doing God's work. With joy without and joy within, all is well.

JANET ERSKINE STUART

Live for today but hold your hands open to tomorrow.
Anticipate the future and its changes with joy. There is a seed
of God's love in every event, every circumstance,
every unpleasant situation in which you may find yourself.

BARBARA JOHNSON

Life itself, every bit of health that we enjoy, every hour of liberty
and free enjoyment…comes from the hand of God.

BILLY GRAHAM

The joy of the LORD is your strength.

NEHEMIAH 8:10 NLT

Hills and Valleys

How blessed all those in whom you live,
whose lives become roads you travel;
They wind through lonesome valleys,
come upon brooks, discover cool springs
and pools brimming with rain! God-traveled,
these roads curve up the mountain,
and at the last turn—Zion! God in full view!

PSALM 84:5–7 MSG

All our supply is to come from the Lord.
Here are springs that shall never dry; here are fountains
and streams that shall never be cut off. Here, anxious one,
is the gracious pledge of the Heavenly Father.
If He is the source of our mercies they can never fail us.
No heat, no drought can parch that river
"the streams whereof make glad the city of God."

N. L. ZINZENDORF

God's ways seem dark, but soon or late,
They touch the shining hills of day.

JOHN GREENLEAF WHITTIER

The LORD your God is bringing you into a good land
of flowing streams and pools of water, with fountains
and springs that gush out in the valleys and hills.

DEUTERONOMY 8:6–7 NLT

Keep trying. It's only from the valley that the mountain seems high.

All We Need

God takes care of His own. He knows our needs.... He stands
ready to come to our rescue. And at just the right moment He
steps in and proves Himself as our faithful heavenly Father.

CHARLES R. SWINDOLL

All who listen to me will live in peace, untroubled by fear of harm.

PROVERBS 1:33 NLT

When we are in a situation where Jesus is all we have,
we soon discover He is all we really need.

GIGI GRAHAM TCHIVIDJIAN

We're depending on GOD; he's everything we need.
What's more, our hearts brim with joy since
we've taken for our own his holy name.

PSALM 33:20 MSG

If you find yourself in this spiritual state feeling wayward,
unstable in heart, confused...cling to the Lord in prayer!
He always hears, and He will answer.

TERESA OF AVILA

When times get hard, remember Jesus.... When tears come,
remember Jesus.... When fear pitches his tent in your
front yard. When death looms, when anger singes,
when shame weighs heavily. Remember Jesus.

MAX LUCADO

Then you will call, and the Lord will answer;
you will cry for help, and he will say: Here am I.

- Isaiah 58:9 NIV

The Father's Heart

All God's glory and beauty come from within, and there He delights to
dwell. His visits there are frequent, His conversation sweet,
His comforts refreshing, His peace passing all understanding.

THOMAS à KEMPIS

There is a place of comfort sweet
Near to the heart of God,
A place where we our Savior meet,
Near to the heart of God....
Hold us who wait before Thee
Near to the heart of God.

CLELAND B. MCAFEE

Now may our Lord Jesus Christ Himself and God our Father,
who has loved us and given us eternal comfort and good hope by grace,
comfort and strengthen your hearts in every good work and word.

2 THESSALONIANS 2:16–17 NASB

Not a sigh is breathed, not a pain felt, not a grief pierces the soul,
but the throb vibrates to the Father's heart.

ELLEN G. WHITE

God comforts. He lays His right hand on the wounded soul…
and He says, as if that one were the only soul in all the universe:
O greatly beloved, fear not: peace be unto you.

AMY CARMICHAEL

I am with you always, even to the end of the age.

MATTHEW 28:20 NKJV

True Comfort

For the LORD God is our sun and our shield.
He gives us grace and glory.
The LORD will withhold no good thing
from those who do what is right.

PSALM 84:11 NLT

After winter comes the summer. After night comes the dawn.
And after every storm, there comes clear, open skies.

SAMUEL RUTHERFORD

Those who sow in tears shall reap in joy.

PSALM 126:5 NKJV

Only God can truly comfort; He comes alongside us
and shows us how deeply and tenderly He feels for us.

Blessed be the God and Father of our Lord Jesus Christ,
the Father of mercies and God of all comfort,
who comforts us in all our affliction so that we will be able
to comfort those who are in any affliction with the comfort
with which we ourselves are comforted by God.

2 CORINTHIANS 1:3–4 NASB

Grace…like the Lord, the Giver, never fails from age to age.

JOHN NEWTON

He won't brush aside the bruised and the hurt
and he won't disregard the small and insignificant.

ISAIAH 42:3 MSG

God's Compassion

He shall gather the lambs with his arm, and carry them in his bosom (Isaiah 40:11 NKJV). Who is He of whom such gracious words are spoken? He is the Good Shepherd. Why does He carry the lambs in His bosom? Because He has a tender heart, and any weakness at once melts His heart. The sighs, the ignorance, the feebleness of the little ones of His flock draw forth His compassion.

CHARLES H. SPURGEON

Because of the LORD's great love
we are not consumed,
for his compassions never fail.
They are new every morning;
great is your faithfulness.
I say to myself, "The LORD is my portion;
therefore I will wait for him."
The LORD is good to those whose hope is in him,
to the one who seeks him;
it is good to wait quietly
for the salvation of the LORD.

LAMENTATIONS 3:22–26 NIV

The LORD!
The God of compassion and mercy!
I am slow to anger
and filled with unfailing love and faithfulness.
I lavish unfailing love to a thousand generations.

EXODUS 34:6–7 NLT

*he loving God we serve has immeasurable compassion
and tenderness toward each of us throughout our lives.*

JAMES DOBSON

Desperate Faith

The faith for desperate days. The Bible is full of such days.
Its record is made up of them, its songs are inspired by them,
its prophecy is concerned with them, and its revelation has come
through them. The desperate days are the stepping-stones
in the path of light. They seem to have been God's
opportunity and man's school of wisdom.

S. CHADWICK

Consider it pure joy, my brothers,
whenever you face trials of many kinds.

JAMES 1:2 NIV

Difficulties and obstacles are God's challenges to faith.
When hindrances confront us in the path of duty,
we are to recognize them as vessels for faith to fill with
the fullness and all-sufficiency of Jesus; and as we go forward,
simply and fully trusting Him, we may be tested,
we may have to wait and let patience have her perfect work;
but we shall surely find at last the stone rolled away and the Lord
waiting to render to us double for our time of testing.

A. B. SIMPSON

Remember it is the very time for faith to work when sight ceases.
The greater the difficulties, the easier for faith; as long as there
remain certain natural prospects, faith does not get on even
as easily as where natural prospects fail.

GEORGE MÜELLER

My God shall supply all your need according to His riches in glory by Christ Jesus.

Tower of Strength

Hear my cry, O God;
Give heed to my prayer.
From the end of the earth I call to You when my heart is faint;
Lead me to the rock that is higher than I.
For You have been a refuge for me,
A tower of strength against the enemy.
Let me dwell in Your tent forever;
Let me take refuge in the shelter of Your wings.

PSALM 61:1–4 NASB

When God has become…our refuge and our fortress,
then we can reach out to Him in the midst of a broken
world and feel at home while still on the way.

HENRI J. M. NOUWEN

I have set the LORD always before me;
because He is at my right hand I shall not be moved.

PSALM 16:8 KJV

I know not where His islands lift their fronded palms in air;
I only know I cannot drift beyond His love and care.

JOHN GREENLEAF WHITTIER

Should we feel at times disheartened…, a simple movement of heart
toward God will renew our powers. Whatever He may demand of us,
He will give us at the moment the strength and courage that we need.

FRANÇOIS FÉNELON

*Weak as we are
a strength beyond our strength has pulled us through
at least this far.*

FREDERICK BUECHNER

Seek His Face

See God in everything, and God will calm and color all that you see!
It may be that the circumstances of our sorrows will not be removed,
their condition will remain unchanged; but if Christ, as Lord and
Master of our life, is brought into our grief and gloom, "He will
compass us about with songs of deliverance" (Psalm 32:7 KJV). To see
Him, and to be sure that His wisdom cannot err, His power cannot
fail, His love can never change; to know that even His direst dealings
with us are for our deepest spiritual gain, is to be able to say, in the
midst of bereavement, sorrow, pain, and loss, "The Lord gave, and the
Lord has taken away; blessed be the name of the Lord" (Job 1:21 KJV).

HANNAH WHITALL SMITH

Look to the LORD and his strength;
seek his face always.
Remember the wonders he has done.

PSALM 105:4–5 NIV

Do you have a place of shelter where you seek only His face? Do you
spend time in that secret place? Have you given prayer the priority it
deserves? When you pray, remember it is the Lord's face you seek.

CHARLES R. SWINDOLL

Look to the Lord and his strength;
seek his face always.
Remember the wonders he has done.

PSALM 105:4–5 NIV

My heart says of you, "Seek his face!"
Your face, LORD, I will seek.

PSALM 27:8 NIV

One night I dreamed I was walking
Along the beach with the Lord.
Many scenes from my life flashed across the sky.
In each scene I noticed footprints in the sand.
Sometimes there were two sets of footprints.
Other times there was one set of footprints.
This bothered me because I noticed that
During the low periods of my life when I was
Suffering from anguish, sorrow, or defeat,
I could see only one set of footprints,
So I said to the Lord, "You promised me,

You promised me.

Lord, that if I followed You,
You would walk with me always.
But I noticed that during the most trying periods
Of my life there have only been
One set of prints in the sand.
Why, when I have needed You most,
You have not been there for me?"
The Lord replied,
"The times when you have seen
only one set of footprints
Is when I carried you."

By Faith

Great faith isn't the ability to believe long
and far into the misty future. It's simply taking
God at His word and taking the next step.

JONI EARECKSON TADA

Now faith is being sure of what we hope
for and certain of what we do not see....
By faith we understand that the universe
was formed at God's command, so that what
is seen was not made out of what was visible....
And without faith it is impossible to please God,
because anyone who comes to him
must believe that he exists and that he
rewards those who earnestly seek him.

HEBREWS 11:1, 3, 6 NIV

Faith goes up the stairs that love has made
and looks out the window which hope has opened.

CHARLES H. SPURGEON

Faith is not exactly belief. One can believe anything...
it's an assent in the mind. But faith is
completely different. It's the actual active
engagement of *God* in one's personal life.

BRIAN STILLER

Let us draw near to God with a sincere heart in full assurance of faith.... Let us hold unswervingly to the hope we profess, for he who promised is faithful.

HEBREWS 10:22–23 NIV

Perfect Peace

Do not let your heart be troubled; believe in God, believe also in Me.
In My Father's house are many dwelling places; if it were not so,
I would have told you; for I go to prepare a place for you.
If I go and prepare a place for you, I will come again and receive
you to Myself, that where I am, there you may be also.... I will not
leave you as orphans; I will come to you.... Peace I leave with you;
My peace I give to you; not as the world gives do I give to you.
Do not let your heart be troubled, nor let it be fearful.

JOHN 14:1–3, 18, 27 NASB

You will keep in perfect peace
him whose mind is steadfast,
because he trusts in you.
Trust in the LORD forever,
for the LORD, the LORD, is the Rock eternal.

ISAIAH 26:3–4 NIV

Let's praise His name! He is holy, He is almighty. He is love.
He brings hope, forgiveness, heart cleansing, peace and power.
He is our deliverer and coming King. Praise His wonderful name!

LUCILLE M. LAW

Therefore, since we have been made right in God's sight
by faith, we have peace with God because of what
Jesus Christ our Lord has done for us.

ROMANS 5:1 NLT

The God of peace gives perfect peace to those whose hearts are stayed upon Him.

CHARLES H. SPURGEON

Renewing Promises

Into all our lives, in many simple, familiar, homely ways,
God infuses this element of joy from the surprises of life,
which unexpectedly brighten our days, and fill our eyes with light.

SAMUEL LONGFELLOW

Each time a rainbow appears, stretching from one end of the sky
to the other, it's God renewing His promise. Each shade of color,
each facet of light displays the radiant spectrum
of God's love—a promise that life can be new for each one of us.

Brightness of my Father's glory,
Sunshine of my Father's face,
Let Your glory e'er shine on me,
Fill me with Your grace.

JEAN SOPIAN PIGOTT

In keeping with his promise we are looking forward
to a new heaven and a new earth.

2 PETER 3:13 NIV

It doesn't take a huge spotlight to draw attention to how great our God is.
All it takes is for one committed person to so let His light shine before men,
that a world lost in darkness welcomes the light.

GARY SMALLEY AND JOHN TRENT

God's touch...lights the world with color and renews our hearts with life.

JANET L. WEAVER SMITH

*Every good and perfect gift is from above, coming down from
the Father of the heavenly lights, who does not change like shifting shadows.*

JAMES 1:17 NIV

Faithfulness Extended

Remember your promise to me;
it is my only hope.
Your promise revives me;
it comforts me in all my troubles....
Your eternal word, O LORD,
stands firm in heaven.
Your faithfulness extends to every generation,
as enduring as the earth you created.

PSALM 119:49–50, 52, 54–55, 89–91 NLT

There are times, and there will be times,
when it will be absolutely clear that only God's grace
keeps us from falling apart; and even if we cannot
hold on to Him, He will still hold on to us.

JOHANNES FACIUS

I will praise you, O LORD, among the nations;
I will sing of you among the peoples.
For great is your love, reaching to the heavens;
your faithfulness reaches to the skies.
Be exalted, O God, above the heavens;
let your glory be over all the earth.

PSALM 57:9–11 NIV

Swim through your troubles. Run to the promises, they are our Lord's branches hanging over the water so that His children may take a grip of them.

SAMUEL RUTHERFORD

A New Day

A new day rose upon me. It was as if another sun had risen into the sky;
the heavens were indescribably brighter, and the earth fairer; and that day
has gone on brightening to the present hour. I have known the other joys
of life…but it is certain that till we see God in the world—God in the bright
and boundless universe—we never know the highest joy.

ORVILLE DEWEY

In the morning, O LORD, You will hear my voice;
in the morning I will order my prayer to You and eagerly watch.

PSALM 5:3 NASB

With God, life is eternal—both in quality and length. There is no joy
comparable to the joy of discovering something new from God, about God.
If the continuing life is a life of joy, we will go on discovering, learning.

EUGENIA PRICE

Always new. Always exciting. Always full of promise.
The mornings of our lives, each a personal daily miracle!

GLORIA GAITHER

That is God's call to us—simply to be people who are content
to live close to Him and to renew the kind of life in which
the closeness is felt and experienced.

THOMAS MERTON

A quiet morning with a loving God puts the events
of the upcoming day into proper perspective.

JANETTE OKE

*Satisfy us in the morning with your unfailing love,
that we may sing for joy and be glad all our days.*

PSALM 90:14 NIV

Promised Strength

Our feelings do not affect God's facts.
They may blow up, like clouds, and cover the eternal
things that we do most truly believe.
We may not see the shining of the
promises—but they still shine! [His strength] is not
for one moment less because of our human weakness.

AMY CARMICHAEL

In Your hand is power and might;
In Your hand it is to make great
And to give strength to all.

1 CHRONICLES 29:12 NKJV

In his kindness God called you to share in his eternal
glory by means of Christ Jesus. So after you have suffered
a little while, he will restore, support, and strengthen you,
and he will place you on a firm foundation.

1 PETER 5:10 NLT

God has not promised skies always blue,
flower-strewn pathways all our lives through;
God has not promised sun without rain,
joy without sorrow, peace without pain.
But God has promised strength for the day,
rest for the labor, light for the way,
grace for the trials, help from above,
unfailing sympathy, undying love.

ANNIE JOHNSON FLINT

God's promises are like the stars; the darker the night the brighter they shine.

DAVID NICHOLAS

Promise Keeper

For as the rain comes down, and the snow from heaven,
and do not return there, but water the earth, and make it bring forth
and bud, that it may give seed to the sower and bread to the eater,
so shall My word be that goes forth from My mouth;
it shall not return to Me void, but it shall accomplish what I please,
and it shall prosper in the thing for which I sent it.

ISAIAH 55:10–11 NKJV

The LORD always keeps his promises;
he is gracious in all he does.
The LORD helps the fallen
and lifts those bent beneath their loads.
The eyes of all look to you in hope....
The LORD is righteous in everything he does;
he is filled with kindness.
The LORD is close to all who call on him,
yes, to all who call on him in truth.

PSALM 145:13–15, 17–18 NLT

Therefore know that the LORD your God, He is God,
the faithful God who keeps covenant
and mercy for a thousand generations with those
who love Him and keep His commandments.

DEUTERONOMY 7:9 NKJV

God is the God of promise. He keeps His word,
even when that seems impossible.

COLIN URQUHART

Not one word has failed of all His good promise.

1 KINGS 8:56 NASB

In His Hands

God promises to keep us in the palm of His hand,
with or without our awareness.
God has already made a space for us,
even if we have not made a space for God.

DAVID AND BARBARA SORENSEN

From eternity to eternity I am God.
No one can snatch anyone out of my hand.
No one can undo what I have done.

ISAIAH 43:13 NLT

Into Your hands, O Lord, we commend
ourselves this day. Let Your presence
be with us to its close. Strengthen us to remember
that in whatsoever good work we do we are serving You.
Give us a diligent and watchful spirit,
that we may seek in all things to know Your will,
and knowing it, gladly to perform it,
to the honor and glory of Your name;
through Jesus Christ our Lord.

GELASIAN SACRAMENTARY

Behold, I have inscribed you on the palms of My hands.

ISAIAH 49:16 NASB

God...holds your entire life—body and soul—in his hands.

LUKE 12:5 MSG

Transformed

To pray is to change. This is a great grace. How good of God to provide a path whereby our lives can be taken over by love and joy and peace and patience and kindness and goodness and faithfulness and gentleness and self-control.

RICHARD J. FOSTER

Create in me a clean heart, O God, and renew a steadfast spirit within me.

PSALM 51:10 NKJV

For God is, indeed, a wonderful Father who longs
to pour out His mercy upon us, and whose majesty is so great
that He can transform us from deep within.

TERESA OF AVILA

The full power of the Word lies…in its transforming power
that does its divine work as we listen. It is a word to heal us through,
and in, our listening here and now.

HENRI J. M. NOUWEN

Be transformed by the renewing of your mind, that you may prove
what is that good and acceptable and perfect will of God.

ROMANS 12:2 NKJV

A life transformed by the power of God is always a marvel and a miracle.

GERALDINE NICHOLAS

Anyone who belongs to Christ has become a new person.
The old life is gone; a new life has begun!

2 CORINTHIANS 5:17 NLT

Unfailing Promises

Jesus Christ opens wide the doors of the treasure house
of God's promises, and bids us go in and take
with boldness the riches that are ours.

CORRIE TEN BOOM

Not one word of all the good words which
the LORD your God spoke concerning you has failed;
all have been fulfilled for you, not one of them has failed.

JOSHUA 23:14 NASB

The fulfillment of God's promise depends entirely
on trusting God and his way, and then simply
embracing him and what he does.
God's promise arrives as pure gift.

ROMANS 4:16 MSG

Your promises have been thoroughly tested;
that is why I love them so much.

PSALM 119:140 NLT

We may…depend upon God's promises, for…He will be
as good as His word. He is so kind that He cannot deceive us,
so true that He cannot break His promise.

MATTHEW HENRY

Faith in God is not blind. It is based on His character and His promises.

One night I dreamed I was walking
Along the beach with the Lord.
Many scenes from my life flashed across the sky.
In each scene I noticed footprints in the sand.
Sometimes there were two sets of footprints.
Other times there was one set of footprints.
This bothered me because I noticed that
During the low periods of my life when I was
Suffering from anguish, sorrow, or defeat,
I could see only one set of footprints,
So I said to the Lord, "You promised me,

You would walk with me.

Lord, that if I followed You,
You would walk with me always.
But I noticed that during the most trying periods
Of my life there have only been
One set of prints in the sand.
Why, when I have needed You most,
You have not been there for me?"
The Lord replied,
"The times when you have seen
only one set of footprints
Is when I carried you."

Step by Step

My Lord God, I have no idea where I am going.
I do not see the road ahead of me. I cannot know
for certain where it will end.... But I believe that
the desire to please You does in fact please You.
And I hope I have that desire in all that I am doing.
I hope that I will never do anything apart from that desire.
And I know that if I do this, You will lead me
by the right road though I may know nothing about it.
Therefore will I trust You always though I may seem
to be lost and in the shadow of death. I will not fear,
for You are ever with me. And You will never
leave me to face my perils alone.

THOMAS MERTON

This is the kind of life you've been invited into,
the kind of life Christ lived. He suffered everything
that came his way so you would know that it could be done,
and also know how to do it, step-by-step.

1 PETER 2:21 MSG

Faith is meant to be lived moment by moment. It isn't some
broad, general outline—it's a long walk with a real Person.

JONI EARECKSON TADA

I would rather walk with God in the dark than go alone in the light.

MARY GARDINER BRAINARD

Yet I am always with you; you hold me by my right hand.

PSALM 73:23 NIV

Guided by His Hand

To You, O LORD, I lift up my soul.
O my God, in You I trust....
Make me know Your ways,
O LORD; teach me Your paths.
Lead me in Your truth and teach me,
for You are the God of my salvation;
for You I wait all the day.
Remember, O LORD, Your compassion
and Your lovingkindnesses,
for they have been from of old.

PSALM 25:1–2, 4–6 NASB

We are of such value to God that He came to live
among us...and to guide us home. He will go to any length
to seek us, even to being lifted high upon the cross to draw us back
to Himself. We can only respond by loving God for His love.

CATHERINE OF SIENA

You guide me with your counsel,
leading me to a glorious destiny.

PSALM 73:24 NLT

The Lord is able to guide. The promises cover
every imaginable situation....
Take the hand He stretches out.

ELISABETH ELLIOT

For this God is our God for ever and ever; he will be our guide even to the end.

PSALM 48:14 NIV

House of Peace

Your walk with God is essential. His heart is not seen
in an occasional chat or weekly visit. We learn His will
as we take up residence in His house every single day.

MAX LUCADO

Those who know Your name will put their trust in You;
for You, LORD, have not forsaken those who seek You.

PSALM 9:10 NKJV

God came to us because God wanted to join us
on the road, to listen to our story, and to help
us realize that we are not walking in circles
but moving toward the house of peace and joy.

HENRI J. M. NOUWEN

The fruit of the Spirit is love, joy,
peace, patience, kindness, goodness,
faithfulness, gentleness and self-control.

GALATIANS 5:22–23 NIV

The thought of You stirs us so deeply that
we cannot be content unless we praise You,
because You have made us for Yourself
and our hearts find no peace until they rest in You.

AUGUSTINE

*Surely goodness and mercy shall follow me all the days of my life;
and I will dwell in the house of the LORD forever.*

PSALM 23:6 NKJV

Personal Guide

I'll take the hand of those who don't know the way,
who can't see where they're going. I'll be a personal
guide to them, directing them through unknown country.
I'll be right there to show them what roads to take,
make sure they don't fall into the ditch. These are
the things I'll be doing for them—sticking with them,
not leaving them for a minute.

ISAIAH 42:16 MSG

Whether you turn to the right or to the left,
your ears will hear a voice behind you,
saying, "This is the way; walk in it."

ISAIAH 30:21 NIV

May God's love guide you through
the special plans He has for your life.

The LORD says, "I will guide you along the best pathway for your life.
I will advise you and watch over you."

PSALM 32:8 NLT

Heaven often seems distant and unknown,
but if He who made the road…is our guide,
we need not fear to lose the way.

HENRY VAN DYKE

We can make our plans, but the LORD determines our steps.

PROVERBS 16:9 NLT

Perfect Faithfulness

I know that God is faithful. I know that He answers prayers,
many times in ways I may not understand.

SHEILA WALSH

O LORD, You are my God;
I will exalt You, I will give thanks to Your name;
For You have worked wonders,
Plans formed long ago, with perfect faithfulness.

ISAIAH 25:1 NASB

Let us, with a gladsome mind,
Praise the Lord, for He is kind:
For His mercies aye endure,
Ever faithful, ever sure.

JOHN MILTON

You, O Lord, are a compassionate and gracious God,
slow to anger, abounding in love and faithfulness.

PSALM 86:15 NIV

God takes care of His own. He knows our needs.
He anticipates our crises. He is moved by our weaknesses.
He stands ready to come to our rescue. And at just the right moment
He steps in and proves Himself as our faithful heavenly Father.

CHARLES R. SWINDOLL

Let love and faithfulness never leave you;
bind them around your neck,
write them on the tablet of your heart.

PROVERBS 3:3 NIV

I will declare that your love stands firm forever,
that you established your faithfulness in heaven itself.

PSALM 89:2 NIV

Blessing on Blessing

Bless the LORD, O my soul;
And all that is within me, bless His holy name!
Bless the LORD, O my soul,
And forget not all His benefits:
Who forgives all your iniquities,
Who heals all your diseases,
Who redeems your life from destruction,
Who crowns you with lovingkindness and tender mercies,
Who satisfies your mouth with good things,
So that your youth is renewed like the eagle's.

PSALM 103:1–5 NKJV

God is a rich and bountiful Father, and He does not
forget His children, nor withhold from them anything
which it would be to their advantage to receive.

J. K. MACLEAN

I will send down showers in season;
there will be showers of blessing.

EZEKIEL 34:26 NIV

We benefit eternally by God's being just what He is.

From the fullness of his grace we have
all received one blessing after another.

JOHN 1:16 NIV

God, who is love—who is, if I may say it this way, made out of love—simply cannot help but shed blessing on blessing upon us.

HANNAH WHITALL SMITH

Stony Paths

Our trials are great opportunities. Too often we
look on them as great obstacles. It would be a haven
of rest and an inspiration of unspeakable power
if each of us from now on would recognize every
difficult situation as one of God's chosen ways
of proving to us His love and look around for
the signals of His glorious manifestations; then,
indeed, would every cloud become a rainbow
and every mountain a path of ascension
and a scene of transfiguration.

A. B. SIMPSON

Each of us may be sure that if God sends us on stony paths
He will provide us with strong shoes, and He will not send us
out on any journey for which He does not equip us well.

ALEXANDER MACLAREN

I will go before you and make the rough places smooth;
I will shatter the doors of bronze and cut through their iron bars.

ISAIAH 45:2 NASB

His love has no limit, His grace has no measure,
His power no boundary known unto men;
For out of His infinite riches in Jesus
He giveth and giveth and giveth again.

ANNIE JOHNSON FLINT

Every valley shall be filled in, every mountain and hill made low.
The crooked roads shall become straight, the rough ways smooth.

LUKE 3:5 NIV

True Peace

To be glad of life, because it gives you
the chance to love and to work and to play
and to look up at the stars; to be satisfied
with your possessions, but not contented
with yourself until you have made
the best of them...to think seldom
of your enemies, often of your friends,
and every day of Christ; and to spend
as much time as you can, with body
and with spirit in God's out-of-doors—these
are little guideposts on the footpath to peace.

HENRY VAN DYKE

Clothe yourselves with love, which binds us all
together in perfect harmony. And let the peace
that comes from Christ rule in your hearts.

COLOSSIANS 3:15 NLT

Only God gives true peace—a quiet gift He sets within us
just when we think we've exhausted our search for it.

Give me the peace that comes from knowing that where I am,
You are, and together we can handle whatever comes.

PAM KIDD

In his unfailing love, my God will stand with me.
He will let me look down in triumph on all my enemies.

PSALM 59:10 NLT

But now the LORD my God has given me peace on every side...and all is well.

1 KINGS 5:4 NLT

Blessing on the Way

All perfect gifts are from above
and all our blessings show
The amplitude of God's dear love
which any heart may know.

LAURA LEE RANDALL

Blessed are all who fear the LORD,
who walk in his ways.

PSALM 128:1 NIV

Many of the richest blessings which have
come down to us from the past are the fruit
of sorrow or pain. We should never forget
that redemption, the world's greatest blessing,
is the fruit of the world's greatest sorrow.

MILLER

Give away your life; you'll find life given back,
but not merely given back—given back with
bonus and blessing. Giving, not getting, is the way.

LUKE 6:38 MSG

Strength, rest, guidance, grace, help, sympathy,
love—all from God to us! What a list of blessings!

EVELYN STENBOCK

Give thanks for unknown blessings already on their way.

NATIVE AMERICAN PROVERB

One night I dreamed I was walking
Along the beach with the Lord.
Many scenes from my life flashed across the sky.
In each scene I noticed footprints in the sand.
Sometimes there were two sets of footprints.
Other times there was one set of footprints.
This bothered me because I noticed that
During the low periods of my life when I was
Suffering from anguish, sorrow, or defeat,
I could see only one set of footprints,
So I said to the Lord, "You promised me,

During the most trying periods.

Lord, that if I followed You,
You would walk with me always.
But I noticed that during the most trying periods
Of my life there have only been
One set of prints in the sand.
Why, when I have needed You most,
You have not been there for me?"
The Lord replied,
"The times when you have seen
only one set of footprints
Is when I carried you."

Quieting the Tumult

I will let God's peace infuse every part of today.
As the chaos swirls and life's demands
pull at me on all sides, I will breathe in
God's peace that surpasses all understanding.
He has promised that He would set within
me a peace too deeply planted to be affected
by unexpected or exhausting demands.

WENDY MOORE

Calm me, O Lord, as You stilled the storm,
Still me, O Lord, keep me from harm.
Let all the tumult within me cease,
Enfold me, Lord, in Your peace.

CELTIC TRADITIONAL

Don't fret or worry. Instead of worrying, pray.
Let petitions and praises shape your worries
into prayers, letting God know your concerns.
Before you know it, a sense of God's wholeness,
everything coming together for good, will come
and settle you down. It's wonderful what happens
when Christ displaces worry at the center of your life.

PHILIPPIANS 4:6–7 MSG

God cannot give us a happiness and peace apart from Himself,
because it is not there. There is no such thing.

C. S. LEWIS

Nothing in all creation is so like God as stillness.

MEISTER ECKART

Our Gracious God

The LORD longs to be gracious to you; he rises to show you compassion.
For the LORD is a God of justice. Blessed are all who wait for him!

ISAIAH 30:18 NIV

His overflowing love delights to make us partakers
of the bounties He graciously imparts.

HANNAH MORE

O LORD, be gracious to us; we long for you.
Be our strength every morning, our salvation in time of distress.

ISAIAH 33:2 NIV

GOD makes everything come out right;
he puts victims back on their feet....
He doesn't treat us as our sins deserve,
nor pay us back in full for our wrongs.
As high as heaven is over the earth,
so strong is his love to those who fear him.
And as far as sunrise is from sunset,
he has separated us from our sins.

PSALM 103:6, 9–12 MSG

That God can bring good out of our mistakes is part
of the wonder of His gracious sovereignty.
The Jesus who restored Peter after His denial
and corrected His course more than once after
that is our Savior today and He has not changed.

J. I. PACKER

Lord…give me only Your love and Your grace.
With this I am rich enough, and I have no more to ask.

IGNATIUS OF LOYOLA

Whom Shall I Fear?

The LORD is my light and my salvation—
whom shall I fear?
The LORD is the stronghold of my life—
of whom shall I be afraid?…
One thing I ask of the LORD, this is what I seek:
that I may dwell in the house of the LORD
all the days of my life,
to gaze upon the beauty of the LORD
and to seek him in his temple.
For in the day of trouble
he will keep me safe in his dwelling;
he will hide me in the shelter of his tabernacle
and set me high upon a rock….
Hear my voice when I call, O LORD;
be merciful to me and answer me.

PSALM 27:1, 4–5, 7 NIV

When I can run to Jesus, when He is my refuge,
strength, and comforter, why would I fear anything?
There is no need for fear.
He is watching over me and that sets my heart at peace.

I will sing about your power.
Each morning I will sing with joy about your unfailing love.
For you have been my refuge,
a place of safety when I am in distress.

PSALM 59:16 NLT

*Leave behind your fear and dwell on the lovingkindness of God,
that you may recover by gazing on Him.*

BERNARD OF CLAIRVAUX

Touch of Joy

Joy is the touch of God's finger. The object of our
longing is not the touch but the Toucher.
This is true of all good things—they are all God's touch.
Whatever we desire, we are really desiring God.

PETER KREEFT

The godly will rejoice in the LORD
and find shelter in him.
And those who do what is right
will praise him.

PSALM 64:10 NLT

Every person's life is a fairy tale written by God's fingers.

HANS CHRISTIAN ANDERSEN

Joy is really a road sign pointing us to God.
Once we have found God…we no longer need
to trouble ourselves so much about the quest for joy.

C. S. LEWIS

I will greatly rejoice in the Lord; my soul will exult in my God,
for He has clothed me with the garments of salvation;
He has wrapped me with a robe of righteousness.

ISAIAH 61:10 NASB

May the God of hope fill you with all joy and peace in believing.

ROMANS 15:13 NKJV

Lift My Eyes

I will lift up my eyes to the hills—
from whence comes my help?
My help comes from the LORD,
who made heaven and earth.
He will not allow your foot to be moved;
He who keeps you will not slumber.
Behold, He who keeps Israel
Shall neither slumber nor sleep.
The LORD is your keeper;
the LORD is your shade at your right hand.
The sun shall not strike you by day,
nor the moon by night.
The LORD shall preserve you from all evil;
He shall preserve your soul.
The LORD shall preserve
your going out and your coming in
from this time forth, and even forevermore.

PSALM 121:1–8 NKJV

Lift up your eyes. Your heavenly Father waits to bless you—in inconceivable
ways to make your life what you never dreamed it could be.

ANNE ORTLUND

I lift up mine eyes to the quiet hills,
and my heart to the Father's throne;
in all my ways, to the end of days,
the Lord will preserve His own.

TIMOTHY DUDLEY-SMITH

Let us fix our eyes on Jesus...who for the joy set before Him endured the cross...and sat down at the right hand of the throne of God...so that you will not grow weary and lose heart.

HEBREWS 12:2–3 NIV

Forever Joy

Be truly glad! There is wonderful joy ahead.... You love him
even though you have never seen him. Though you do not see him now,
you trust him; and you rejoice with a glorious, inexpressible joy.

1 PETER 1:6, 8–9 NLT

Your deepest joy comes when you have nothing around you
to bring outward pleasure and Jesus becomes your total joy.

A. WETHERELL JOHNSON

The ransomed of the Lord will return. They will enter Zion
with singing; everlasting joy will crown their heads. Gladness and joy
will overtake them, and sorrow and sighing will flee away.

ISAIAH 35:10 NIV

Herein is joy, amid the ebb and flow of the passing world:
our God remains unmoved, and His throne endures forever.

ROBERT COLEMAN

Rejoice always, pray without ceasing, in everything give thanks;
for this is the will of God in Christ Jesus for you.

1 THESSALONIANS 5:16–18 NKJV

Through all eternity to You
a joyful song I'll raise;
for oh! eternity's too short
to utter all Your praise.

JOSEPH ADDISON

As we follow Him who is everlasting we will touch the things that last forever.

Rest in Him

My soul finds rest in God alone;
my salvation comes from him.
He alone is my rock and my salvation;
he is my fortress, I will never be shaken....
My salvation and my honor depend on God;
he is my mighty rock, my refuge.
Trust in him at all times, O people;
pour out your hearts to him,
for God is our refuge....
One thing God has spoken,
two things have I heard:
that you, O God, are strong,
and that you, O Lord, are loving.

PSALM 62:1–2, 7–8, 11–12 NIV

Joy comes from knowing God loves me and knows who I am
and where I'm going...that my future is secure as I rest in Him.

JAMES DOBSON

Rest in the LORD, and wait patiently for him.

PSALM 37:7 NASB

When God finds a soul that rests in Him
and is not easily moved...to this same soul
He gives the joy of His presence.

CATHERINE OF GENOA

He who dwells in the shelter of the Most High will rest in the shadow of the Almighty.

PSALM 91:1 NIV

Guide Us

Incredible as it may seem, God wants our companionship.
He wants to have us close to Him.
He wants to be a father to us, to shield us, to protect us,
to counsel us, and to guide us in our way through life.

BILLY GRAHAM

The LORD will guide you always;
he will satisfy your needs in a sun-scorched land....
You will be like a well-watered garden,
like a spring whose waters never fail.

ISAIAH 58:11 NIV

Abandon yourself to His care and guidance,
as a sheep in the care of a shepherd, and trust Him utterly.

HANNAH WHITALL SMITH

Through the heartfelt mercies of our God,
God's Sunrise will break in upon us...
showing us the way, one foot at a time,
down the path of peace.

LUKE 1:78–79 MSG

Be our strength in hours of weakness,
In our travels be our guide;
Through attempts, failure, danger,
Father, be at our side.

LOVE MARIA WILLIS

*S*ince you are my rock and my fortress,
for the sake of your name lead and guide me.

PSALM 31:2–3 NIV

Fresh Hope

God…rekindles burned-out lives with fresh hope,
restoring dignity and respect to their lives—a place in the sun!
For the very structures of earth are GOD'S;
he has laid out his operations on a firm foundation.

1 SAMUEL 2:7–8 MSG

Do not look forward to the changes and chances
of this life in fear; rather look to them with
full hope that, as they arise, God, whose you are,
will deliver you out of them.

FRANCIS DE SALES

I will praise you forever for what you have done;
in your name I will hope, for your name is good.
I will praise you in the presence of your saints.

PSALM 52:9 NIV

Blessed are those who trust in the LORD
and have made the LORD their hope and confidence.

JEREMIAH 17:7 NLT

The hope we have in Christ is an absolute certainty.
We can be sure that the place Christ is preparing for
us will be ready when we arrive, because with Him nothing
is left to chance. Everything He promised He will deliver.

BILLY GRAHAM

Though seen through many a tear,
Let not my star of hope grow dim or disappear.

BENJAMIN SCHMOLCK

One night I dreamed I was walking
Along the beach with the Lord.
Many scenes from my life flashed across the sky.
In each scene I noticed footprints in the sand.
Sometimes there were two sets of footprints.
Other times there was one set of footprints.
This bothered me because I noticed that
During the low periods of my life when I was
Suffering from anguish, sorrow, or defeat,
I could see only one set of footprints.
So I said to the Lord, "You promised me,

I have needed You.

Lord, that if I followed You,
You would walk with me always.
But I noticed that during the most trying periods
Of my life there have only been
One set of prints in the sand.
Why, when I have needed You most,
You have not been there for me?"
The Lord replied,
"The times when you have seen
only one set of footprints
Is when I carried you."

Patiently Waiting

God has put into each of our lives a void that cannot be filled by the world. We may leave God or put Him on hold, but He is always there, patiently waiting for us...to turn back to Him.

EMILIE BARNES

You must not forget this one thing, dear friends: A day is like a thousand years to the Lord, and a thousand years is like a day. The Lord isn't really being slow about his promise, as some people think. No, he is being patient for your sake. He does not want anyone to be destroyed, but wants everyone to repent.

2 PETER 3:8–9 NLT

God is waiting for us to come to Him with our needs....
God's throne room is always open.

CHARLES STANLEY

God waits to give to those who ask Him a wisdom that will bind us to Himself, a wisdom that will find expression in a spirit of faith and a life of faithfulness.

J. I. PACKER

Don't you see how wonderfully kind, tolerant, and patient God is with you?... Can't you see that his kindness is intended to turn you from your sin?

ROMANS 2:4 NLT

God waits for us in the inner sanctuary of the soul. He welcomes us there.

RICHARD J. FOSTER

All Is Well

It's usually through our hard times, the unexpected
and not-according-to-plan times, that we experience God
in more intimate ways. We discover an unquenchable longing
to know Him more. It's a passion that isn't concerned that life fall
within certain predictable lines, but a passion that pursues God
and knows He is relentless in His pursuit of each one of us.

WENDY MOORE

A living, loving God can and does make His presence felt,
can and does speak to us in the silence of our hearts,
can and does warm and caress us till we no longer doubt
that He is near, that He is here.

BRENNAN MANNING

In difficulties, I can drink freely of God's power
and experience His touch of refreshment
and blessing—much like an invigorating early spring rain.

ANABEL GILLHAM

Lord, you have been our dwelling place throughout
all generations. Before the mountains were born
or you brought forth the earth and the world,
from everlasting to everlasting you are God.

PSALM 90:1–2 NIV

Before me, even as behind, God is, and all is well.

JOHN GREENLEAF WHITTIER

God Is Good

The goodness of God is infinitely more wonderful
than we will ever be able to comprehend.

A. W. TOZER

All that is good, all that is true, all that is beautiful,
all that is beneficent, be it great or small,
be it perfect or fragmentary, natural as well as supernatural,
moral as well as material, comes from God.

JOHN HENRY NEWMAN

I am still confident in this:
I will see the goodness of the LORD
in the land of the living.
Wait for the LORD;
be strong and take heart
and wait for the LORD.

PSALM 27:13–14 NIV

We walk without fear, full of hope and courage and strength
to do His will, waiting for the endless good which He is always giving
as fast as He can get us able to take it in.

GEORGE MACDONALD

Once you look at the cross, you can't look at anything else,
no matter how horrid it appears, and infer that God's
intention is to do us harm. The truth is that God is good.

WILLIAM BACKUS

....
....
....
....
....
....
....
....
....
....
....
....
....
....
....
....
....
....

Open your mouth and taste, open your eyes and see—how good GOD is. Blessed are you who run to him. Worship GOD if you want the best; worship opens doors to all his goodness.

PSALM 34:8–9 MSG

Known by Him

The simple fact of being…in the presence of the Lord and of showing Him all that I think, feel, sense, and experience, without trying to hide anything, must please Him. Somehow, somewhere, I know that He loves me, even though I do not feel that love as I can feel a human embrace, even though I do not hear a voice as I hear human words of consolation.… God is greater than my senses, greater than my thoughts, greater than my heart. I do believe that He touches me in places that are unknown even to myself.

HENRI J. M. NOUWEN

But He knows the way I take;
When He has tried me, I shall come forth as gold.

JOB 23:10 NASB

Pour out your heart to God your Father.
He understands you better than you do.
It is in silence that God is known,
and through mysteries that He declares Himself.

ROBERT H. BENSON

This is your Father you are dealing with,
and he knows better than you what you need.
With a God like this loving you, you can pray very simply.

MATTHEW 6:7 MSG

If anyone loves God, this one is known by Him.

1 CORINTHIANS 8:3 NKJV

Immeasurable Love

You are valuable just because you exist. Not because of what you
do or what you have done, but simply because you are.
Just think about the way Jesus honors you...and smile.

MAX LUCADO

We have come to know and have believed
the love which God has for us. God is love,
and the one who abides in love abides
in God, and God abides in him.

1 JOHN 4:16 NASB

You, O God, are both tender and kind,
not easily angered, immense in love,
and you never, never quit.

PSALM 86:15 MSG

In His love He clothes us, enfolds us,
and embraces us; that tender love completely
surrounds us, never to leave us.

JULIAN OF NORWICH

God in His ample love embraces our
love with...a sort of tenderness, and we must
tread the Way to Him hand in hand.

SHELDON VANAUKEN

For God so loved the world that he gave his one and only Son, that whoever believes in him shall not perish but have eternal life.

JOHN 3:16 NIV

Good Plans

"For I know the plans I have for you," declares the LORD,
"plans to prosper you and not to harm you,
plans to give you hope and a future."

JEREMIAH 29:11 NIV

Even when all we see are the tangled threads
on the backside of life's tapestry,
we know that God is good and is out to do us good always.

RICHARD FOSTER

No eye has seen, no ear has heard, no mind has conceived
what God has prepared for those who love him.

1 CORINTHIANS 2:9 NIV

You are no stranger to God. He planned for you…from before
the foundation of the world, and His plan was to be with you.
And He invites you to realize it, to come into a continual awareness
of His presence and be revolutionized by it.

RAY AND ANNE ORTLUND

God specializes in things fresh and firsthand.
His plans for you this year may outshine those of the past….
He's preparing to fill your days with reasons to give Him praise.

JONI EARECKSON TADA

The counsel of the LORD stands forever,
The plans of His heart from generation to generation.

PSALM 33:11 NASB

Wayside Rest

Know you not that day follows night, that flood
comes after ebb, that spring and summer succeed winter?
Hope you then! Hope you ever! God fails you not.

CHARLES H. SPURGEON

God provides resting places as well as working places. Rest, then,
and be thankful when He brings you, wearied to a wayside well.

L. B. COWMAN

In those times I can't seem to find God,
I rest in the assurance He knows how to find me.

NEVA COYLE

This is what the LORD says:
"Stand at the crossroads and look;
ask for the ancient paths,
ask where the good way is, and walk in it,
and you will find rest for your souls."

JEREMIAH 6:16 NIV

Rest. Rest in God's love. The only work you are required now to do
is to give your inmost intense attention to His still, small voice within

MADAME JEANNE GUYON

As for me, I trust in You, O LORD.
I say, "You are my God.
My times are in Your hand."

PSALM 31:14–15 NASB

God's peace is joy resting. His joy is peace dancing.

F. F. BRUCE

Unclear Moments

Perhaps this moment is unclear,
but let it be—even if the next, and many
moments after that are unclear, let them be.
Trust that God will help you work them out,
and that all the unclear moments will
bring you to that moment of clarity
and action when you are known by Him
and know Him. These are the better
and brighter moments of His blessing.

WENDY MOORE

The temptations in your life are no different
from what others experience. And God is faithful.
He will not allow the temptation to be more than
you can stand. When you are tempted,
he will show you a way out so that you can endure.

1 CORINTHIANS 10:13 NLT

Give me a word, O Word of the Father:
touch my heart:
enlighten the understandings of my heart:
open my lips and fill them with Your praise.

LANCELOT ANDREWES

If any of you lacks wisdom, let him ask of God, who gives to all generously and without reproach, and it will be given to him.

JAMES 1:5 NASB

His Faithful Love

Show the wonder of your great love....
Keep me as the apple of your eye;
hide me in the shadow of your wings.

PSALM 17:7–8 NIV

All the things in this world are gifts and signs of God's love to us.
The whole world is a love letter from God.

PETER KREEFT

Give thanks to the LORD, for he is good!
His faithful love endures forever.
Give thanks to the God of gods.
His faithful love endures forever.
Give thanks to the Lord of lords.
His faithful love endures forever.

PSALM 136:1–3 NLT

At the very heart and foundation of all God's dealings with us,
however dark and mysterious they may be, we must dare to believe
in and assert the infinite, unmerited, and unchanging love of God.

The LORD is merciful and compassionate,
slow to get angry and filled with unfailing love....
The LORD always keeps his promises
He is gracious in all he does.

PSALM 145:8, 13 NLT

There is the whisper of His love, the joy of His presence,
and the shining of His face, for those who love Jesus for Himself alone.

SUSAN B. STRACHAN

O Lord God Almighty, who is like you? You are mighty,
O Lord, and your faithfulness surrounds you.

PSALM 89:8 NIV

One night I dreamed I was walking
Along the beach with the Lord.
Many scenes from my life flashed across the sky.
In each scene I noticed footprints in the sand.
Sometimes there were two sets of footprints.
Other times there was one set of footprints.
This bothered me because I noticed that
During the low periods of my life when I was
Suffering from anguish, sorrow, or defeat,
I could see only one set of footprints,
So I said to the Lord, "You promised me,

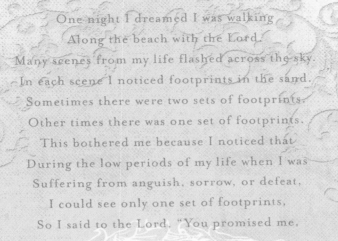

I carried you.

Lord, that if I followed You,
You would walk with me always.
But I noticed that during the most trying periods
Of my life there have only been
One set of prints in the sand.
Why, when I have needed You most,
You have not been there for me?"
The Lord replied,
"The times when you have seen
only one set of footprints
Is when I carried you."

Reassuring Presence

Know by the light of faith that God is present,
and be content with directing all your actions toward Him.

BROTHER LAWRENCE

Let the healing grace of Your love, O Lord, so transform me that I may play
my part in the transfiguration of the world from a place of suffering...to a
realm of infinite light, joy, and love. Make me so obedient to Your Spirit that
my life may become a living prayer and a witness to your unfailing presence.

MARTIN ISRAEL

Where can I go from your Spirit?
Where can I flee from your presence?
If I go up to the heavens, you are there;
if I make my bed in the depths, you are there.
If I rise on the wings of the dawn,
if I settle on the far side of the sea,
even there your hand will guide me,
your right hand will hold me fast.

PSALM 139:7–10 NIV

O Lord God, in whom we live, and move, and have our being,
open our eyes that we may behold Your fatherly presence ever about us.
Draw our hearts to Yourself with the power of Your love.

BROOKE FOSS WESTCOTT

Look for, long for, pray for, and expect special breaking-through times
when God makes His presence very real, very powerful! And until they come,
dwell in His presence by faith and gaze upon His beauty.

RAY AND ANNE ORTLUND

I am with you and will watch over you wherever you go.

GENESIS 28:15 NIV

God's Power

I pray that you, being rooted and established in love,
may have power, together with all the saints,
to grasp how wide and long and high
and deep is the love of Christ, and to know this love
that surpasses knowledge—
that you may be filled to the measure of all the fullness of God.
Now to him who is able to do immeasurably more
than all we ask or imagine, according to his power that is at
work within us, to him be glory in the church and in Christ Jesus
throughout all generations, for ever and ever!
Amen.

EPHESIANS 3:17–21 NIV

God longs to give favor—that is, spiritual strength
and health—to those who seek Him, and Him alone.
He grants spiritual favors and victories...in order to make
His holy beauty and His great redeeming power known.

THERESA OF AVILA

Faith is the bucket of power lowered
by the rope of prayer into the well of God's abundance.
What we bring up depends upon what we let down.
We have every encouragement to use a big bucket.

VIRGINIA WHITMAN

God is working in you, giving you the desire and the power to do what pleases him.

PHILIPPIANS 2:13 NLT

Guided by Grace

God guides us, despite our uncertainties
and our vagueness, even through our failings
and mistakes…. He leads us step by step,
from event to event. Only afterwards,
as we look back over the way we have come
and reconsider certain important moments
in our lives in the light of all that has followed them,
or when we survey the whole progress of our lives,
do we experience the feeling of having been led
without knowing it, the feeling that
God has mysteriously guided us.

PAUL TOURNIER

Let us then approach the throne of grace
with confidence, so that we may receive mercy
and find grace to help us in our time of need.

HEBREWS 4:16 NIV

Among our treasures are such wonderful things as the grace of Christ,
the love of Christ, the joy and peace of Christ.

L. B. COWMAN

Today Jesus is working just as wonderful works as when
He created the heaven and the earth. His wondrous grace,
His wonderful omnipotence, is for His child who needs
Him and who trusts Him, even today.

CHARLES E. HURLBURT AND T. C. HORTON

They travel lightly whom God's grace carries.

THOMAS à KEMPIS

Close to His Heart

The LORD is my shepherd;
I shall not want.
He makes me to lie down in green pastures;
He leads me beside the still waters.
He restores my soul;
He leads me in the paths of righteousness
For His name's sake.
Yea, though I walk through the valley of the shadow of death,
I will fear no evil; for You are with me;
Your rod and Your staff, they comfort me.
You prepare a table before me in the presence of my enemies;
You anoint my head with oil; my cup runs over.
Surely goodness and mercy shall follow me
All the days of my life:
And I will dwell in the house of the LORD
Forever.

PSALM 23:1–6 NKJV

In comparison with this big world, the human heart is only
a small thing. Though the world is so large, it is utterly unable
to satisfy this tiny heart. Our ever growing soul and its capacities
can be satisfied only in the infinite God. As water is restless until
it reaches its level, so the soul has no peace until it rests in God.

SADHU SUNDAR SINGH

He tends his flock like a shepherd:
He gathers the lambs in his arms
and carries them close to his heart.

ISAIAH 40:11 NIV

I am the good shepherd. The good shepherd gives His life for the sheep.

JOHN 10:11 NKJV

Most Dear

The God who created, names, and numbers the stars
in the heavens also numbers the hairs of my head.... He pays
attention to very big things and to very small ones. What matters
to me matters to Him, and that changes my life.

ELISABETH ELLIOT

In all their distress he too was distressed,
and the angel of his presence saved them.
In his love and mercy he redeemed them;
he lifted them up and carried them all the days of old.

ISAIAH 63:9 NIV

What matters supremely is not the fact that I know God,
but the larger fact which underlies it—the fact that He knows me.
I am graven on the palms of His hands. I am never out of His mind.
All my knowledge of Him depends on His sustained initiative
in knowing me. I know Him because He first knew me,
and continues to know me.

J. I. PACKER

God has a wonderful plan for each person He has chosen.
He knew even before He created this world what beauty
He would bring forth from our lives.

LOUISE B. WYLY

You're blessed when you feel you've lost what is most dear to you.
Only then can you be embraced by the One most dear to you.

MATTHEW 5:4 MSG

Ever Present

God walks with us.... He scoops us up in His arms or simply
sits with us in silent strength until we cannot avoid the awesome
recognition that yes, even now, He is here.

GLORIA GAITHER

I will remember that when I give Him my heart,
God chooses to live within me—body and soul. And I know
He really is as close as breathing, His very Spirit inside of me.

There's not a tint that paints the rose
Or decks the lily fair,
Or marks the humblest flower that grows,
But God has placed it there....
There's not a place on earth's vast round,
In ocean's deep or air,
Where love and beauty are not found,
For God is everywhere.

God is our refuge and strength, an ever-present help in trouble.
Therefore we will not fear.

PSALM 46:1–2 NIV

At every moment, God is calling your name and waiting to be found.
To each cry of "Oh Lord," God answers, "I am here."

God is the sunshine that warms us, the rain that melts the frost
and waters the young plants. The presence of God is a climate
of strong and bracing love, always there.

JOAN ARNOLD

You have made known to me the path of life; you will fill me with joy in your presence, with eternal pleasures at your right hand.

PSALM 16:11 NIV

Chosen and Loved

Tonight I will sleep beneath Your feet,
O Lord of the mountains and valleys,
ruler of the trees and vines. I will rest
in Your love, with You protecting me
as a father protects his children,
with You watching over me
as a mother watches over her children.

We have been in God's thought from all eternity,
and in His creative love, His attention never leaves us.

MICHAEL QUOIST

Long before he laid down earth's foundations,
he had us in mind, had settled on us
as the focus of his love.... It's in Christ that
we find out who we are and what
we are living for. Long before
we first heard of Christ and got our
hopes up, he had his eye on us,
had designs on us for glorious living.

EPHESIANS 1:4, 11 MSG

When we allow God the privilege of shaping our lives,
we discover new depths of purpose and meaning.
What a joyful thought to realize you are a chosen
vessel for God—perfectly suited for His use.

JONI EARECKSON TADA

God's way is perfect. All the LORD's promises prove true.
He is a shield for all who look to him for protection.

PSALM 18:30 NLT

Surround Me

The light of God surrounds me,
The love of God enfolds me....
The presence of God watches over me,
Wherever I am, God is.

God's love is meteoric,
his loyalty astronomic,
His purpose titanic,
his verdicts oceanic.
Yet in his largeness
nothing gets lost.

PSALM 36:5 MSG

He is everything that is good and comfortable for us.
He is our clothing that for love wraps us, clasps us,
and all surrounds us for tender love.

JULIAN OF NORWICH

What can harm us when everything must first touch
God whose presence surrounds us?

The LORD is my strength and my shield;
my heart trusted in Him, and I am helped.

PSALM 28:7 NKJV

The Lord doesn't always remove the sources of stress
in our lives...but He's always there and cares for us.
We can feel His arms around us on the darkest night.

JAMES DOBSON

The eternal God is your refuge, and underneath are the everlasting arms.

DEUTERONOMY 33:27 NKJV

Perfect Love

Nothing enters your life accidently—remember that.
Behind our every experience is our loving, sovereign God.

CHARLES R. SWINDOLL

In this way, love is made complete among us so that we will have
confidence on the day of judgment, because in this world we are like him.
There is no fear in love. But perfect love drives out fear.

1 JOHN 4:17–18 NIV

With God our trust can be abandoned, utterly free. In Him are
no limitations, no flaws, no weaknesses. His judgment is perfect,
His knowledge of us is perfect, His love is perfect. God alone is trustworthy.

EUGENIA PRICE

He is the Rock, his works are perfect,
and all his ways are just.
A faithful God who does no wrong,
upright and just is he.

DEUTERONOMY 32:4 NIV

There is no need to plead that the love of God shall fill our hearts as though
He were unwilling to fill us.... Love is pressing around us on all sides like air.
Cease to resist it and instantly love takes possession.

AMY CARMICHAEL

May you experience the love of Christ, though it is too great to understand fully. Then you will be made complete with all the fullness of life and power that comes from God.

EPHESIANS 3:19 NLT

He Will Carry You

I've called your name. You're mine.
When you're in over your head, I'll be there with you.
When you're in rough waters, you will not go down.
When you're between a rock and a hard place,
it won't be a dead end—
Because I am GOD, your personal God,
The Holy of Israel, your Savior.
I paid a huge price for you…!
That's how much you mean to me!
That's how much I love you!

ISAIAH 43:1–4 MSG

In His arms He carries you all day long.

FANNY J. CROSBY

The LORD your God is with you, he is mighty to save.
He will take great delight in you, he will quiet you with His love,
he will rejoice over you with singing.

ZEPHANIAH 3:17 NIV

Look back from where we have come…. How could we know the joy
without the suffering? And how could we endure the suffering
but that we are warmed and carried on the breast of God?

DESMOND M. TUTU

The more we depend on God the more dependable we find He is.

CLIFF RICHARD

You carry us, and You go before, You are the journey, and the journey's end.

BOETHIUS

A PREMIER JOURNAL

© 2010 by Ellie Claire Gift & Paper Corp.
Minneapolis 55438
www.ellieclaire.com

Compiled by Marilyn Jansen
Designed by Lisa & Jeff Franke

Scripture references are from the following sources: The Holy Bible, New International Version®
NIV®. © 1973, 1978, 1984 by Biblica, Inc.™ Used by permission of Zondervan. The New King James
Version (NKJV). Copyright © 1982 by Thomas Nelson, Inc. Used by permission. All rights reserved
worldwide. The Holy Bible, New Living Translation (NLT). Copyright © 1996, 2004. Used by
permission of Tyndale House Publishers, Inc., Wheaton, Illinois 60189. THE MESSAGE (MSG) © 1993,
1994, 1995, 1996, 2000, 2001, 2002 by Eugene Peterson. Used by permission of NavPress, Colorado
Springs, CO. The New American Standard Bible® (NASB), Copyright © 1960, 1962, 1963, 1968, 1971,
1972, 1973, 1975, 1977, 1995 by The Lockman Foundation. Used by permission. All rights reserved.

Excluding Scripture verses and deity pronouns, in some quotations references to men and masculine
pronouns have been replaced with gender-neutral or feminine references. Additionally, in some
quotations we have carefully updated verb forms and wordings that may distract modern readers.

ISBN 978-1-60936-034-4

Printed in China.